CHECKERBOARD SOCIAL STUDIES LIBRARY

CHARACTER COUNTS

RESPONSIBILITY COUNTS

by Marie Bender

Reviewed by
Dr. Howard Kirschenbaum, Ed.D.

ABDO
Publishing Company

visit us at
www.abdopub.com

Published by ABDO Publishing Company, 4940 Viking Drive, Edina, Minnesota 55435. Copyright © 2003 by Abdo Consulting Group, Inc. International copyrights reserved in all countries. No part of this book may be reproduced in any form without written permission from the publisher.

Printed in the United States.

Photo credits: BananaStock Ltd., Brand X Pictures, Comstock, Corbis Images, Digital Vision, PhotoDisc, Rubberball Productions, Skjold Photography, Stockbyte

Editors: Kate A. Conley, Stephanie Hedlund

Design and production: Mighty Media

Library of Congress Cataloging-in-Publication Data

Bender, Marie, 1968-
    Responsibility counts / Marie Bender.
       p. cm. -- (Character counts)
    Summary: Defines responsibility as a character trait and discusses how to show respect at home, with friends, at school, in the community, and toward oneself.
    Includes bibliographical references (p.) and index.
    ISBN 1-57765-874-4
    1. Responsibility--Juvenile literature. [1. Responsibility.] I. Title.

BJ1451 .B46 2002
179' .9--dc21

2002074531

Internationally known educator and author Howard Kirschenbaum has worked with schools, non-profit organizations, governmental agencies, and private businesses around the world to develop school/family/community relations and values education programs for more than 30 years. He has written more than 20 books about character education, including a high school curriculum. Dr. Kirschenbaum is currently the Frontier Professor of School, Family, and Community Relations at the University of Rochester and teaches classes in counseling and human development.

CONTENTS

CHARACTER COUNTS

*Parents can only give good advice or put them on the right
paths, but the final forming of a person's character lies in
their own hands.* —Anne Frank, holocaust victim and author

Your character is the combination of **traits** that makes you an individual. It's not your physical traits, such as the color of your eyes or how tall you are. Rather, character is your thoughts, feelings, beliefs, and values.

Your character shows in the way you interact with your family, friends, teachers, and other community members. People who are well liked and successful are said to have a good character. Many traits build good character. Some of these traits include caring, fairness, honesty, good citizenship, responsibility, and respect.

Good Citizenship

Responsibility

Respect

Honesty

Fairness

Caring

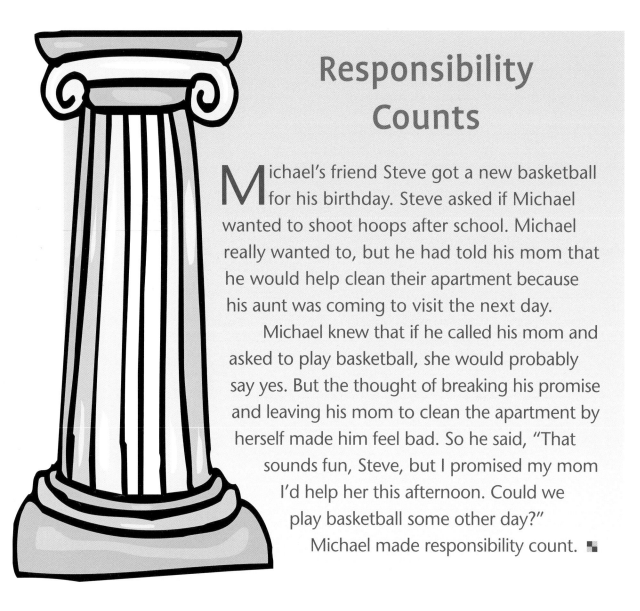

Responsibility Counts

Michael's friend Steve got a new basketball for his birthday. Steve asked if Michael wanted to shoot hoops after school. Michael really wanted to, but he had told his mom that he would help clean their apartment because his aunt was coming to visit the next day.

Michael knew that if he called his mom and asked to play basketball, she would probably say yes. But the thought of breaking his promise and leaving his mom to clean the apartment by herself made him feel bad. So he said, "That sounds fun, Steve, but I promised my mom I'd help her this afternoon. Could we play basketball some other day?"

Michael made responsibility count.

WHAT IS RESPONSIBILITY?

You can't escape the responsibility of tomorrow by evading it today. —Abraham Lincoln, sixteenth president of the United States

Responsibility means doing what is right, keeping your promises, and acting **appropriately**. It means fulfilling your **obligations** and doing your duty. Responsible people are honest, trustworthy, and dependable. And when they do something wrong, they admit their mistakes and do what they can to make it right. Following the rules and trying to make good choices are also part of being responsible.

Your actions and choices all have **consequences**. Some consequences are good, such as getting a good grade because you chose to study and as a result did well on a test. Other **consequences** are bad, such as being grounded because you broke the rules by throwing a ball in the house and breaking a lamp. Being responsible means you try to have as many good consequences and as few bad consequences as possible.

Being responsible does not mean being perfect. You are human and will sometimes make mistakes or poor choices. A responsible person tries not to purposely hurt others by his or her words or actions. As long as you try to do your best, accept the consequences, and learn from your mistakes, you are acting responsibly.

List the choices you have made recently and their consequences.

Did you have more good or bad consequences?

What could you have done differently to avoid the bad consequences?

RESPONSIBILITY

Making Choices

 Think about what you want to do and what the consequences will be before you do it.

 Gather all the information you can about the choice you need to make.

 Consider all of the possible choices for the situation.

 Weigh the positive and negative parts of each choice.

 Make a decision about what to do based on the facts and your sense of right and wrong.

 Accept responsibility for the choices you make.

RESPONSIBILITY

11

RESPONSIBILITY AND FAMILY

Any man's life will be filled with constant and unexpected encouragement if he makes up his mind to do his level best each day.
—Booker T. Washington, educator

Each member of a family has responsibilities. Your parents love you, and it is their responsibility to take care of you. They give you food, shelter, and clothing. They make sure you go to school, help you discover your talents, and take you to a doctor when you are sick. As a

member of your family, you are responsible to help out around the house, follow the rules, and treat family members with respect.

If you have younger **siblings**, helping care for them may be a part of your responsibilities. For example, you can hold your little brother's hand when crossing the street. Or you can play with your baby sister while your parents make dinner.

Other responsibilities may include clearing the table, washing the dishes, or cleaning your room. You might also be responsible for feeding and walking the dog, or taking out the trash. Doing these things without being reminded, and without arguing, complaining, or waiting until the last minute, is part of being responsible.

Another part of being responsible is being honest and keeping your word. When you tell your parents you are going to a friend's house after school, then that is where you go. If you tell your mom you will be home in time for dinner, then make sure you are not late. The more you keep your word, the more freedom your parents will give you because they will trust you.

You can keep your word to your **siblings**, too. For example, if you told your sister you would play with her, do not change your plans if your friends later ask you to go in-line skating. Your family members depend on you, so you must be honest with your friends about your

Think about it…

Are you honest with your parents about where you go and what you do when you are not with them?

How do you feel when you do not keep your promises to family members?

responsibilities. Most likely, your friends can wait for you, or reschedule an activity for another time. Being honest, dependable, and reliable are all parts of being responsible.

RESPONSIBILITY AND FRIENDS

I long to accomplish some great and noble task, but it is my chief duty to accomplish small tasks as if they were great and noble.

—Helen Keller, Nobel Prize winner, social activist, public speaker, and author

Friendship involves responsibility. Most of the time, friendships are fun. But there can also be misunderstandings, anger, or hurt feelings. Being a good friend means taking responsibility for your part in the friendship. If you say something hurtful that you did not mean, it is your responsibility to own up to your behavior and apologize to your friend. It is not easy to say you were at fault, but you will feel better about your mistake.

In the same way, when friends speak badly about you or cancel plans to do something else, it is their

responsibility to admit to their mistake and apologize. Friends learn from their mistakes and try not to act the same hurtful way again toward each other.

Unlike your parents, school, and community, your friends do not have the authority to make rules or laws for you to follow. Your responsibilities to your friends are to be honest with them and keep your promises. People want to be friends with people they know they can count on. Your friends know they can count on you to return things you borrow from them. They know that if you say you will meet them after school at 4:00, then you will be there at 4:00, not 4:15 or 4:30.

Friends trust and rely on each other. They turn to each other when they have problems because they trust each other to be there. You and your friend both need to take responsibility for making your friendship work. For example, if you are always the one to invite your friend over or to do favors for your friend, then you may start to feel used. Each friend should offer invitations and go out of his or her way to help the other.

> **Think about it...**
>
> *When was the last time you had a fight with a friend?*
>
> *Did you apologize to each other and make up?*

RESPONSIBILITY AND SCHOOL

My philosophy is that not only are you responsible for your life, but doing the best at this moment puts you in the best place for the next moment. —Oprah Winfrey, TV talk show host

B eing responsible at school means following the rules. The rules help make your school a safe place for everybody to learn. If no one followed the rules, teachers would spend their time trying to keep order instead of teaching. It is every student's responsibility to respect and follow the rules.

The reason you go to school is to learn. It is your teacher's responsibility to teach you what you need to know to succeed. It is your responsibility to listen to your teachers and do your best on your assignments and tests. You are responsible for turning in your homework on time and for asking questions if you do not understand.

If for some reason you don't do an assignment, don't make excuses or tell lies about it. Tell your teacher that you are sorry you didn't

What would your school be like if no one followed the rules?

What do you think would happen?

do the work and ask if you can have more time to finish it, or if you can do a make-up assignment. You will probably get a lower grade, but that is the **consequence** of not fulfilling your responsibility.

You also have responsibilities to others in your school. These responsibilities include treating people respectfully and helping in the classroom. It is your responsibility not to disrupt class or make it hard for your classmates to learn. If you are working on a group project, it is your

responsibility to do your share of the work. You are also responsible for returning library materials on time and keeping your desk or locker neat.

When you act responsibly, others are likely to follow your example. When everyone is responsible, it creates a less stressful environment and promotes learning.

RESPONSIBILITY

RESPONSIBILITY
AND COMMUNITY

For the nation's rise and fall every citizen has a responsibility.

—Chinese proverb

In your community, it is your responsibility to obey laws and treat your neighbors with respect. Laws make your community safe for everyone. It is your responsibility to report unusual things to an adult. If something in your neighborhood needs to be fixed or if someone is hurting someone else, you should tell an adult so he or she can help.

Being responsible means respecting your neighbors' property as well your community's public areas. This means not riding your bike through people's yards and not letting your dog dig in someone's garden. It also means playing ball in the park rather than in your yard so you won't break windows or dent cars.

It is also your responsibility to be respectful of the environment. This means you do not litter, and

> **Think about it...**
>
> *How can you show the people in your community that you are responsible?*

you pick up trash you see lying around and throw it away properly. It also means you do not harm, chase, or tease animals.

Community responsibility also means getting involved and **participating** in neighborhood activities. You can do this through a local community center, a youth group, or organizations such as Boy Scouts, Girl Scouts, or Boys & Girls Clubs of America. Your parents can help you find programs that are available in your area. When you get involved in activities and organizations, you learn to understand the importance of community responsibility.

RESPONSIBILITY AND YOU

We cannot do everything at once, but we can do something at once. —Calvin Coolidge, thirtieth president of the United States

Sometimes it's hard not to get caught up in your responsibilities. The most important responsibility to yourself is taking care of your health. You can do this by eating healthily, getting enough sleep, exercising, brushing your teeth, and bathing or showering regularly. You should also tell your parents or the school nurse if you don't feel well so they can help you get better.

It's also important to do things you enjoy so that everything you do doesn't feel like a chore. Having a hobby that you enjoy improves

your mental and emotional health. If you aren't happy and healthy, you won't be able to fulfill the responsibilities to yourself or to others.

You also have a responsibility to think about your future. This means doing your best at school so you can get a good education. It means thinking about the kind of person you want to be. It also means trying to achieve your **potential** in areas such as sports or music. Finding things to do that you are good at helps you develop confidence. When you have confidence in yourself, you feel more able to do what you are supposed to do.

Finally, you have a responsibility to be true to yourself. You can do this by being honest with yourself and others. You can follow your **conscience** and always try to do what you think is right. When you are true to yourself, you feel good about who you are, and that helps you be a more responsible person.

Think about it...

What have you done recently that is good for your health?

What is your favorite thing to do for fun?

What do you do to be responsible to yourself?

MANAGING YOUR RESPONSIBILITIES

Our duty is to be useful, not according to our desires, but according to our powers. —Henry F. Amiel, poet and essayist

Being responsible may seem **overwhelming**. There may be so much you are supposed to do, it may seem that you will never get it all done. Or you might feel like you never have time to relax. But there are things you can do to make your responsibilities more manageable.

First, reduce your responsibilities. Some things you have to do, such as your schoolwork and chores. But other responsibilities are **optional**. You may have many after-school activities. Once you agree to **participate**, you have made a commitment, and following through is your responsibility. But, if you choose not to participate in an activity, then that is one less responsibility. Being responsible does not mean saying yes to every opportunity. It means picking a few things that you really want to do, and then sticking with them until they are done.

Second, improve your organizational skills. If you are often late or forget things, then being organized will keep your responsibilities from seeming frustrating. Start by getting a calendar so you can write down what you need to do each day. Use the calendar to keep track of school assignments, after-school activities, plans with friends, and family commitments. Once you get in the habit of using a calendar, you will be able to spend more time doing what you enjoy.

When you manage your responsibilities well, you show that you know your limits. It

Think about it...

Do your responsibilities sometimes seem overwhelming?

If so, what things could you choose not to do without breaking a commitment?

What do you do to stay organized?

means you set **priorities** so you fulfill your responsibilities the best you can and don't end up with more responsibilities than you have time for. Standing up for yourself and being responsible for your own decisions develops good leadership qualities for both now and for the future.

RESPONSIBILITY

The Golden Rule
Around the World

Hurt not others in ways that you yourself would find hurtful. —Buddha

So whatever you wish that men would do to you, do so to them; for this is the law and the prophets. —*The Gospel of Matthew*

Do not do to others what you do not want them to do to you. —Confucius

Do naught unto others which would cause you pain if done to you. —*The Mahabarata*

No one of you is a believer until he desires for his brother that which he desires for himself. —Muhammad

What is hateful to you, do not to your fellow man. —*The Talmud*

Regard your neighbor's gain as your own gain, and your neighbor's loss as your own loss. —Tai Shang Kan Ying P'ien

Glossary

appropriate - suitable for an occasion; fitting; proper.

conscience - an understanding of right and wrong that encourages a person to do what is right.

consequence - something that results from an earlier action or happening; outcome.

obligation - a binding power, as of a law, promise, or sense of duty.

optional - left to one's choice; not required or automatic.

overwhelming - overpowering or crushing.

participate - to take part or have a share with others, as in an activity or quality.

potential - capable of being or becoming; possible, but not actual.

priority - the condition of coming before another or others, as in order of importance.

sibling - a brother or sister.

trait - a quality that distinguishes one person or group from another.

Web Sites

Would you like to learn more about character? Please visit www.abdopub.com to find up-to-date Web site links about caring, fairness, honesty, good citizenship, responsibility, and respect. These links are routinely monitored and updated to provide the most current information available.

INDEX

For the Character Counts series, ABDO Publishing Company researched leading character education resources and references in an effort to present accurate information about developing good character and why doing so is important. While the title of the series is Character Counts, these books do not represent the Character Counts organization or its mission. ABDO Publishing Company recognizes and thanks the numerous organizations that provide information and support for building good character in school, at home, and in the community.